Messages And Miracles From The Other Side

Thank you for Being a part of the Miracle!

Love, Dolly

Messages And Miracles From The Other Side

Kelly MacLeod

ENCHANTED PRESS
www.enchantedpress.com

FIRST EDITION
First Printing, 2007

Cover design by Wayne J. MacLeod
Title Art by Wayne J. MacLeod
Photographs by Kelly MacLeod
or provided by their respective families.
Book Design and Editing by Lisa Martino

ISBN 978-0-9798995-0-8

If you are unable to order this book from your local bookseller, you may order directly from the publisher.

Call 1.888. 535. 5948 - Toll Free

Enchanted Press
54204 E. Annsbury Cir.
Shelby Twp., MI 48316
586.323.0444

www.enchantedpress.com
www.kellymacleod.com

Printed on acid-free paper in the United States of America

This book is dedicated to my best friend, Natalie, who was my very own personal cheerleader and always encouraged me to follow my passion … and to all of my loved ones that are on the other side guiding and watching over me during my wonderful spiritual journey.

Natalie Krajdub

Sara & Charlie Posey

Mamie & Henry Shrum

Acknowledgements

I would like to thank my wonderful husband, Wayne, for everything that he does for me, and for the fact that he always listens tirelessly to the wonderful experiences that I have with the Spirit World. Without him and his support, I wouldn't be where I am today.

I would like to thank my parents for bringing me into this world and to the rest of my family – all of whom painstakingly listen to me and my stories even when they'd rather not!

I want to thank each and every client for allowing me the wonderful opportunity to connect them with their loved ones and for the lessons that I have learned from the Spirit World through the numerous readings that I have done for them.

I would like to thank my editor, Lisa Martino, for all of her hard work in helping me with the creation of this book. Without her, this book would not be in your hands today. Thank you, Lisa, for the being the enlightened person that you are!

I would like to thank Heather Krentler, "Marketing Guru Extraordinaire" for literally walking into my office and into my life. Thank you for taking a chance, making me your "project" and for being just as passionate about marketing as I am about helping the world!

Last but not least, I would like to give thanks to God/Goddess and the Spirit World for allowing me to represent them and tell their stories as they were told to me.

Contents

When referencing a higher power, for the purpose of this book, I will use the name "God." You may interpret this reference as your own highest spiritual being, be it the Goddess, Creator, The Universe, etc.

Introduction

How It Started

I tell people that everyone is born with psychic ability, gut instinct, intuition or whatever you want to call it. The difference is in deciding whether you want to train it and tap into it — and most of all, trust it.

I was born in 1969 on Detroit's east side and was raised in a non-practicing Baptist household. Growing up, I didn't have much exposure to anything dealing with psychic phenomenon or the paranormal, but when I was a small child, I remember feeling the presence of others and talking to imaginary friends. I now understand that those friends were not "imaginary" at all.

Looking back, I remember my first significant clairvoyant experience happening when I was 13 years-old.

The "in" thing to do back then was to wear jeans that were so tight, you would pretty much had to lay down on the bed in order to get them zipped. And if they still weren't tight enough for you, you would soak the front of them with water and "fry" them in the dryer — the tighter the better!

So, on what seemed like just another day at the bungalow-style house I shared with my mother and sister in a quiet, northeastern Detroit suburb, I wet down the front of my jeans to tighten them and headed off to use our dryer.

As I was running down the basement stairs I had a vision in which I saw myself tumbling head over heels down the stairs until I landed screaming at the bottom of them. I then saw myself shaking off the shock from of the tumble and going on my way to school, unharmed.

Moments later, I snapped out of it and realized that I was fine – and that I had *not* just fallen down the stairs – I remember thinking *"That's horrible! Why would you ever let yourself think something like that?"*

As I headed out the door to school a little while later, I rounded the corner to the stairs, I lost my footing and I began tumbling down the stairs – exactly the same way that I had envisioned it!

While it was happening, I told myself *"I've already done this once, and I was fine. So, just relax and let go,"* and I tumbled head-over-heels down what felt like about 30 steps. When I landed on my back and my head slammed against the solid basement floor, I lay screaming and frightened for a few moments until I assessed that I was probably going to be pretty bruised, but nothing felt broken.

I picked myself up and dusted off (as I did in the vision) and walked to school, running the scenario over again in my mind, still very frightened by what had just happened.

But while I walked, one thought kept coming to mind, and I was really having a hard time letting it go: I kept thinking that I had somehow caused this whole incident because I previously *"thought"* it, and then it came true. For years, I kept the incident to myself for fear that it would be ridiculed.

Of course, today that seems silly to me because I now understand that what really happened to me was what is commonly called "deja'vu" or clairvoyant vision.

I now realize that God allowed me to see what I did in order to prepare me for what was an inevitable situation. Because I had already been shown the outcome, I was able to consciously relax my body as I fell – avoiding a serious injury or even death.

After the premonition about my fall, there were times that similar *"thoughts"* came into my head, but because I was so afraid that I would cause them to manifest, I caused a shut-down of my intuition by denying its power. Eventually, the frequency of these visions lessened, and I began living what was considered a pretty "normal" life. I finished high school, married, and began devoutly frequenting a Pentecostal church and teaching Sunday school in my early 20s.

One Sunday during all of this, my husband at the time was planning to take his motorcycle out for a ride. I told him he should change his clothes into something more appropriate for riding, because I thought that he was going to have an accident. He was wearing sweat pants, a t-shirt, satin jacket, no socks and tennis shoes that weren't tied, but didn't think twice about my warning.

We went our separate ways for the afternoon, and at around 4:10 p.m. as I was out shopping, I felt a thud to my head as though I had been hit with a two-by-four. For a moment, everything went black, and as I regained consciousness, I had a dull, throbbing headache. I was soon to find out that while riding his motorcycle at about 80 miles-per-hour, at 4:10 p.m., he was forced off his bike and slid about 15 feet, with his head stopping only a foot from a telephone pole!

That incident opened the floodgates to visions once again, but at the time I had no knowledge of this type of spirituality, or clairvoyance, or mediums: I just knew that I was getting information ahead of time, and that it was not always positive.

It wasn't until my late 20s that I began to feel restless, as though I was missing something in my life. To feed a sort of spiritual "hunger," I started studying everything in the metaphysical field while working my job at Ford Motor Company. I pretty much devoured every book I could get my hands on that dealt with the paranormal or psychic development; tarot, channeling, angels ... you name it, I was reading it.

I was also awakening to a new understanding of my experiences, but deep down I had an inner battle brewing as I tried to reconcile my hunger for a connection with the metaphysical realm against my ongoing relationship with the Pentecostal religion, which forbade such things. Ironically, I now realize that I was channeling in my church days – accurately quoting scripture I had never seen — but within that religious framework they called it "prophecy."

I soon began taking channeling classes offered in the area by an ordained spiritualist minister who was also a channel and medium, and realized that what I was learning was something that I already knew how to do. The skills came easily, and I learned how to control the natural ability that was already present within me.

Testing the water, I began by doing readings for family and friends. As my confidence grew, I eventually took the plunge into the world of psychic fairs.

The more readings I did, the more I was enjoying this newfound gift. It felt so good to help people! I finally started to realize *this* was what I was searching for and what was really missing in my life.

It wasn't long after I started doing readings in 2000 that both of my grandparents passed away, just two days apart from one another. Right after their passing, I was doing a meditation and asking for my angels, spirit guides and loved ones to connect with me. During this meditation, I asked to have one last time with my grandfather, and I connected with *both* of my grandparents. It was such an amazing event and an overwhelming feeling all at the same time — I just couldn't believe it! That was my first time connecting with what many refer to as the "Other Side."

That day changed my life forever. It was like a healing balm for me, and it left me wanting more. I knew at that moment that I wanted to be able to give the same experience to others, and started focusing more on spirit communication.

In the meantime, the more card readings I did, the sharper my skills became. One day while meditating in my home office, I heard a very loud, booming voice (which I knew was God's voice) and he told me to put away the "crutch," which I interpreted to mean the angel and faerie cards that I used during readings. I had used the cards because I just didn't think I had the skills to be a medium, and besides, I thought every psychic used cards!

Naturally, I was distraught at the command and feeling a little insecure about leaving my "helpers" behind, but after much debate with myself, I started reading without them. When I did, my connections with the "other side" became stronger – I no longer needed tools.

And this is where my journey as a clairvoyant psychic and a medium began.

What It's Like On My Side

When people find out that I'm a full-time psychic, I get a host of reactions that range from positive to negative and everything in between.

There are many misconceptions about psychics. Depending on your religious or spiritual upbringing, I find that psychic ability is considered by many either a "gift" or "work of the Devil."

Most of the time, people either ask me to read their palm (to whom I explain that I don't read palms, and I don't just tell futures). Next are the ones who nervously put their hands over their ears as if classified information is leaking out, and ask me *"Are you reading my mind right now?"* And finally, there are the ones who either do not believe in psychic abilities at all, those who ask me to "cast a spell," or those who look at me with fear in their eyes.

Now, there are some psychics that are always "reading" people (and by that I mean that they are always tapped into someone's energy, getting information about them). However, I abide by the rule that "it's rude to intrude." In other words, if you don't invite me into your energy field, I shouldn't be tapping in without permission.

So, is this profession glamorous or exciting?

People think that being a psychic is one of the greatest jobs in the world, and, I would have to agree with them ... however, it's not because psychics "know everything" and it's not because it always a lot of fun.

I will tell you this: it's definitely not boring! Every day is unique, but it's also filled with a multitude of problems that people have going on in their lives. On an average day, I might help someone cope with the loss of a loved one, a cheating spouse, a loved one's suicide, loss of a job, drug and alcohol addictions – the list goes on and on.

Mentally and emotionally, it is quite draining, because everything involves energy. It takes an incredible amount of my own energy to tune into the energy of several people throughout the day. It takes even more energy to connect and communicate with people that have passed away.

After a while, it can weigh on you and your spirit if you don't learn how to disconnect from your clients' issues. In the beginning, I would take my clients' problems home with me, leaving me overwhelmed.

It wasn't until I came to the conclusion that I'm only here as a messenger, that my job became easier and much more enjoyable. When I realized this, I opened up to the idea that I could help with problems without taking on the energy of the problems themselves.

Whether you like it or not, being a psychic also means that you are thrown into the role of a counselor. You have to learn how to remain objective and very neutral, keeping your own personal feelings and opinions out of the reading.

We also have to be responsible for the information that we give. If I see something that isn't too pleasant ahead, I am still obligated to give the information, but must responsibly communicate that information to the client in a way that does not cause more damage.

I do not edit the information that I receive. If I get it, the client gets it. But, how I choose to present that information will make all the difference in the world. I am here to give guidance, clarity, and a sense of hope to those that are struggling with everyday life. A reading shouldn't leave you feeling upset, devastated or terrified. And you definitely shouldn't believe that you have a curse, evil spirits or a black aura and that you need someone to "fix" it for you for a very hefty price.

With that said, you may be wondering why I choose to keep doing what I do when it can be so taxing to a person on all levels: physically, mentally and emotionally.

Although it's hard to deal with all of the situations and problems on a daily basis, I do get an equal amount of joy and satisfaction out of my job.

When a client walks into my office looking and feeling like they've lost their best friend or say that they just can't make it one more day and they find guidance, empowerment or a sense of peace and comfort, it makes it all worth it. That is what keeps me going each and every day!

I decided to write this book because I want to share all of the wonderful messages, miracles and lessons that have taken place in my own life as well as the lives of my clients in order to reach as many people as I can.

I always tell people that we are all connected like a giant jigsaw puzzle. I can guarantee that if one person is going through a difficult time in his or her life, there are hundreds of others that are experiencing the exact same thing at that very moment.

So many people have questions about life and death, and the other side. Every time I recall the stories and lessons I have experienced, I find that so many others can relate to them, leaving with them with a sense of hope and happiness knowing that they are not alone. That is my hope for you.

When I was a child, I feared my visions and intuition. I now tell people that the only reason you receive information like I did is either to prepare you for what is to come, or to warn you so that you may prevent it from happening.

This book is intended as a vehicle to help people understand how our loved ones connect and communicate similar information with us even after they have physically left the Earth Plane.

My intention is not to persuade you, or change your mind about life and death, but instead I want to share with you the messages and miracles from those that have passed on as they have shared with their loved ones through the thousands of readings that I have done over the years.

With that said, I ask that you keep an open mind as you begin reading my experiences, and as I recall the lessons and readings that go along with them.

Permission has been granted from the individuals whose readings have been used in this book. All actual names have been changed or excluded for the sake of privacy.

As always, all readings are confidential, and remain confidential.

Connecting: How I Do My Readings

Before we get too far into some of my readings, I want to explain how I go about getting the information.

Every psychic does their readings a little differently. There is really no "right" or "wrong" way to do a reading, as long as you are getting the clearest information for the client's greatest and highest good.

My readings are a combination of three elements: I address the most important information going on in a client's life; I focus on questions that they may have that they would like guidance and clarity on; and I communicate with any loved ones that wish to connect with them. I start every day with a prayer to my highest source (God) and ask that I be of the greatest service each and every day, and help as many people as possible. I ask that I receive the highest and finest information for each and every client.

When I sit down with a client, I say a short prayer to myself and ask God, angels, spirit guides and deceased loved ones for the most important and clearest information that the client needs to know at that particular moment – nothing more, nothing less.

At that time, I then begin to tune into the energy of the person that I am sitting with. I tune into their aura for information about the past, present and future.

I am clairvoyant (clear seeing), clairaudient (clear hearing), clairsentient (clear feeling) and also an empath (having the ability to feel physical and emotional experiences of others). So the information comes to me in many different ways, through pictures or small clips like a movie, through sounds or feelings. I tend to experience the reading on all levels physically and emotionally.

I believe that it's my job as a psychic medium and spiritual counselor to provide unbiased insight and guidance in order to help you reach your divine path with minimal bumps and bruises, all while still allowing you to learn all of the lessons that you were meant to learn. My job is also to help facilitate the healing process through spirit communication between you and your loved ones that have passed on.

A deceased loved one may at any time begin connecting and communicating with the client during the reading.

There are several reasons that this may happen. Those that have passed on know that they will have a chance to communicate with their loved one during his or her session with a medium, so when they have the opportunity, they will usually jump at the chance.

People sometimes ask for a guarantee that they will be able to speak to a specific person that has crossed over. My answer to them is this: I can not (nor can any other medium) guarantee that a specific person will definitely make a connection. However, most of the time, we can "send out" for the energy of that person if they don't connect right away. It has been my experience that most of the time, we can get that connection.

Often, if a passing is too "fresh" and the emotions are still very raw, another spirit will connect first to act as a "buffer" in order to prepare the client for the connection.

Sometimes, it's not who we would like to speak to, but who has had the most knowledge and experience in dealing with the situations that you are currently going through that will connect first.

The Law of Free Will

I tell every client the same thing:

- You have the choice to take the information that I am sharing with you and use it as presented, or not.

- You have the choice to take the information and decide it means something different if you don't like what I am telling you.

- You have the choice to disregard the information and continue on the path that you are on.

The information that you are receiving from your reading is not set in stone.

Remember: ultimately, you are in control of your life and your destiny. What you choose to do with the information that you are receiving will change the final outcome of your reading.

I give the information just like I get the information, the information is not "good/positive" or "bad/negative"; it just "is." It is up to you to decide how you would like to handle that information and make the most of the knowledge you receive during your reading.

The following chapters contain stories from over the years, answers to many common questions, and information I have received through the readings I have had the pleasure to do as a medium. Again, I hope it brings you comfort, hope and a greater understanding of the other side.

Enjoy!

PART 1: The Basics

Why Do They Communicate?

Our loved ones continue to connect and communicate with us even after they've passed on. However, most of the time we are so caught up with every day life that we miss the signs and symbols that they are giving us.

People often ask me why they talk to us.

Here are a few answers that I can share with you:

- Sometimes our loved ones just want us to know that they are still around – that just because they are not here on Earth, they are still a part of our lives. They want us to know that they can see what's going on in our life, whether we are happy, sad, angry or frustrated, because they can share in our joys and our heartaches from the Spirit World.
- Our loved ones connect with us to help ease the pain and the loneliness that we feel from their passing.
- They connect with us to help mend relationships – either our relationship with them, or ours with others that are still living here on Earth.
- Sometimes our loved ones connect with us just to say "Hello, I'm OK."
- A loved one will connect because they have the knowledge and wisdom to help you get through a specific situation in life.

But these are just a few reasons I've been given, and I'm sure the list goes on forever.

When Do They Communicate With Us?

People always ask me if it's too soon to connect with a loved one. From my experiences, my answer would have to be: no, it's never too soon or too late to connect with them after they have passed.

I once had a very hurt and grieving young man come for a reading and he connected with his dad. After the reading, I found out that his father had just passed that morning.

Sometimes a loved one will connect during a reading and the client is surprised because they have been gone for a very long time. I usually explain to people that it doesn't matter if it's been one hour or 30 years – there are no limits as to when a person can make contact with us.

Other times, a loved one will connect during a reading and the client will be surprised at who is coming through, especially when they had hoped that another would have connected.

I always tell people that we usually don't get to choose who connects with us, they come on their own because they have the knowledge, guidance and a message to help us get through that period in our life. Or, they may want to talk to us because they want us to give their message to another person that's going through a difficult time.

We can, however, "send out" for the energy of a specific person, and many times we will be successful in connecting with them.

One of the comments I hear from clients whose loved one passed either before they were born or when they were very young, is this:

"I really thought my (Mom/Dad) would have come through during the reading, how come they didn't?"

I then have to explain to them that because they really don't have any of their own experiences or memories with their loved one (because they were never really able to establish a relationship) that even if their loved one did connect, they would not be able to recognize it. Therefore, another person that they are familiar with will come forward to connect instead and sometimes bring messages to them from the other person.

It doesn't solve the hurt that the client feels, but it does help them to understand that in order to connect with a loved one, you have to be able to verify when they do make their connection.

How Our Loved Ones Communicate

Our loved ones continue to connect and communicate with us after they've passed on, however, most of the time we are so caught up with everyday life that we miss the signs and symbols that they are giving us.

You are probably wondering exactly how is it that they communicate, especially when you can't see them or hear them.

The other side connects with us through various signs and symbols, as well as our psychic senses, and especially through our dreams:

- ***Dreams*** – when we are in a dream state, it's easiest for our loved ones to connect with us. It is during that time that we are relaxed and our minds are completely open. Our loved ones know that they can talk to us and interact with us and we will not use our minds to rationalize what we are seeing. Basically, we get out of the way and we don't have anything causing interference, like common issues that go on during our waking hours.

You can tell the difference between a "dream" and a "visit" by the clarity of what you were seeing and sensing. Usually, a dream is kind of foggy or wispy, the details aren't very clear or you will tend to forget the dream after a while.

A visit from your loved one will stay embedded into your mind and your senses for years to come. You will remember details and feelings, almost as if "you were right there with them."

Now, if you have a nightmare about your loved one, it doesn't mean that they are angry or in pain. Usually when we have a nightmare, it's because we feel a sense of remorse or guilt and it displays itself through our dreams.

Other ways our loved ones communicate with us:

- ***Sight*** - we might see repetitive numbers, sometimes it might or might not be a significant date or time. At times it might just be the same number over and over again on a clock, a license plate, the odometer in the car, etc. After a loved one passes away we may also start finding pennies or coins everywhere we go, or feathers that seem to just fall from Heaven.

- ***Sound, Smell & Thoughts*** - we might be thinking about our loved ones and recalling all the happy times that we shared with them, or we might be missing them more than ever and suddenly their favorite song or a song that reminds you of them will come on the radio. Other times, out of nowhere, we might smell their perfume, cigarettes, cigars, pipe smoke or a unique smell that reminds us of them.

Now I know that some of you are thinking *"This happens to me all the time!"* That's right, our loved ones do communicate or at least try to communicate with us, but it's all too easy to dismiss or even miss it all together if we are not paying attention.

I'll give you an example of just how easy it is to miss the signs and symbols they send us, even when you are familiar with their form of communication:

My Visit from Natalie

I was heading to a large festival in Ohio where I would spend the weekend doing individual readings and a group session in which I would connect people with their loved ones that have crossed over. This was a first time event for me and I was very excited, and also kind of nervous. I had a four-hour drive ahead of me and I had so many thoughts running through my head at the time. One thought in particular was of Natalie, my best friend, who had passed away the year before.

All I could think about was the fact that she had always believed in me and the work that I was doing. I was a little teary-eyed thinking that here I am, doing what I love to do, and amazed at how far I had come. I was on my way to do one of the biggest events that I had ever done, and Natalie wasn't even going to be there to see me and share it all.

At that moment, I decided not to think about it anymore, and I reached over to turn the radio on. By chance, the song that happened to be playing was "Lose Yourself," by Eminem. "You better - lose yourself in the music, the moment - You own it, you better never let it go You only get one shot, do not miss your chance to blow. This opportunity comes once in a lifetime" … We always sang this song to each other, especially when we were working together and just "jamming out." Hearing that made me miss her even more.

So, I continued to drive and sing like a rock star, and noticed that in the lane next to me was a Ford Probe. Natalie used to own a Probe. That's weird ... directly in front of me was a Ford Escape in red – just like the car that Natalie had right before she passed. As if that wasn't strange enough, hanging from the rear-view mirror was a stained-glass butterfly ... Natalie always collected angels and butterflies! After nearly being clobbered on the head, it finally dawned on me that Natalie wasn't going to miss my event, she was right there with me, on the way to the festival! She was on the radio, she was in front of me, and she was beside me! Coincidence? Not a chance. I was astounded by the way she decided to tell me that she was there, even if I was a little slow in getting it!

At the festival, I nervously began my group session, worried that the other side wouldn't "show up." However, the energy was strong and I had no trouble at all connecting people with their loved ones. It was amazing – people were laughing and crying – but most of all, people were healing.

After the audience session, one of my friends came up to me and said that when I had first started, he saw this bright "globe" of swirling energy next to me which gently floated away after I got going. There was no doubt in my mind that the energy he happened to see was definitely Natalie, sharing and supporting me at my big event! It was the perfect ending to what I considered a perfect event.

Crossing Over

Many people are worried that if they talk to their loved ones, they will keep them "stuck" here and they won't cross over. That is a myth.

I'd like to take a moment to talk about the difference between those spirits that have crossed over into the light and those that stay stuck here on the Earth Plane.

In my experience as a psychic medium there have been very few occasions when I have read for a client and found that their loved ones have not crossed over into what most of us call "Heaven" or the "afterlife."

Most of the time, a person is very much at peace with their passing and they go willingly to the other side.

When I am connecting with a person that is crossed over, their energy is a lighter, higher vibration than that of a spirit that is still attached here on the Earth Plane, and it's very energizing to me. Even if the spirit communicates and allows me to feel the physical and/or emotional pain that they may be in, it's still more gentle and calm.

At times, I'm asked to participate in paranormal research in order to lend insight to what might be considered a haunting in a commercial or residential location.

During many of those events, I have come across spirits or what some call "ghosts." Regardless of what label you put on them, for some reason, they remain attached to a person or a dwelling here on Earth. Some remain by choice, while others have been willing to cross over with some spiritual guidance.

Their energy usually feels much denser to me. Sometimes the energy will cause me to feel edgy and anxious, or I will experience overwhelming sadness. I have found that when I spend too much time in this energy, I am left feeling very tired or even completely exhausted the following day. It is not the uplifting and positively charged energy like that which comes from those that have crossed over into the light.

Reasons they are "stuck"

The following is what I have learned through some very interesting conversations with those that have passed on who also choose to remain here with us:

- Some die suddenly/unexpectedly, and they didn't realize that they were dead.
- Some are angry for the reasons behind their death, (such as being murdered) and they are not ready to let go of their life here.
- Some have committed suicide and have been taught that they will burn in "Hell" and are so afraid to experience it, that they feel it's better to stay stuck somewhere in the "middle."
- Some do not feel as if they are "worthy" enough to cross over into the light.

- Some feel as if they still have unfinished business to take care of, such as mending relationships.
- In some cases, a person will pass away and they are so comfortable in their surroundings, they just prefer to stay where they are – kind of like being "set" in their ways.

I'm sure there are many other reasons, but we just won't know them until we ask.

Many times, after explaining to the spirit that they have passed on, and that they would be happier if they were to cross over into an environment that offers the unconditional love, healing and nurturing that they deserve, I am able to help them let go of what is keeping them here, allowing them cross over and begin the journey into the light. This is always a refreshing feeling, because you can immediately feel the energy around you change and become much lighter.

Are They My Guardian Angel?

Many people will tell me about significant events in their lives, especially if the event was dangerous and they will state that "________" saved them, and that they just knew that this person was their "guardian angel."

There's a lot of confusion on this topic, and I'd like to talk a little bit about what defines an angel, a spirit guide and a deceased loved one.

Angels – An angel is an entity of the highest vibration that has never been born into a human body before. They can "appear" in human form when needed to lend a hand, but as quickly as they appear, they will also disappear.

An angel's job is to help people by carrying God's unconditional love to them. They also help watch over us and protect us when we need them.

Spirit Guide – A spirit guide is an entity that was born into a physical body and walked the Earth like other human beings.

A spirit guide is hundreds of years old, has learned all of the lessons that s/he was required to learn on Earth, and now resides in spirit form on "the other side."

Since they have learned all of their lessons, spirit guides are now prepared to help us in our endeavors here on Earth. They are prepared with all of the knowledge from their own lessons and know how to best guide us.

Think of our lives and lessons, one day we will have the knowledge to become a spirit guide for someone else here on the Earth Plane. This takes hundreds of years to accomplish, so it would be rare to be a spirit guide for any of our loved ones.

Loved Ones – Our deceased loved ones don't fit into either category; they aren't an angel and they likely haven't been reincarnated long enough to be a spirit guide for us.

However, that doesn't mean that our loved ones don't watch over us. Our loved ones keep tabs on us and can help if we are in a dangerous situation.

PART 2:
The "Other Side" & What They Want You to Know

What it's Like on the Other Side...

The one question that's asked most often is, *"What is it like on the other side?"*

I've found that a description of "the other side" (or what we call Heaven, Nirvana, the afterlife, Shangri-la, Zion, Valhalla, etc.) varies from spirit to spirit. For the purpose, of this discussion, I will refer to it as "Heaven."

First of all, Heaven is what each individual creates in our own minds. (For those of you who are interested in this concept, I recommend watching the Robin Williams film "What Dreams May Come," which illustrates the idea that we create our own Heaven or Hell.)

I've connected with several spirits that have shared their versions of Heaven, and I've been amazed, excited and overjoyed at what each and every one of them has shared with me. I've been told it's the most beautiful place ever; that when they crossed over, they were not contained to a physical body and they could go anywhere at anytime they wanted. Physical, mental and emotional challenges disappeared, and there were no limitations whatsoever!

Those that had immense emotional or physical pain experienced great freedom – or what they say feels like the ultimate bliss – they were finally free of any pain that they may have had in the end or that years leading to their deaths.

Here are some examples of what I've been shown:

Bingo!

One of the very first experiences that I had with a spirit that had crossed over involved a woman who had lived with breast cancer which had eventually spread to all of her major organs. Before she passed, she was in a great amount of pain. When I connected with her, she was wearing a trench coat which she opened as if to "flash" me. She showed me all of the organs which were now a beautiful shimmering gold, conveying to me that all of her organs were 100% healed. I then saw her chain smoking and playing bingo with a big smile on her face.

At the time, I was amazed at this and I thought "What a strange thing to be doing on the other side! Heaven was supposed to be lovely, full of rainbows, sunsets, flowers and the like, wasn't it?" I relayed this information to my client, and she just laughed and said "That sounds just like my mom, she loved to smoke, play bingo and have a good time. What you told me doesn't surprise me at all!"

It was from that moment on that I began to understand that Heaven was going to be different for everyone, depending on what makes each person happiest.

Letting Her Hair Down

On one occasion, a spirit shared with me that here on Earth she identified very much with her ethnic heritage and the old-world values that she had learned as a child.

She was a devoted wife and mother, raising a large family and cooking, cleaning and doing everything right. She never raised her voice or did anything un-ladylike, and was always very "proper."

However, when she passed away she wanted to experience things that she always yearned to try, yet didn't do because she feared the consequences of behaving against expectation and out of character. On this particular day, she showed me that she was having a couple of drinks, smoking and acting a bit rowdy. She told that before she buckled down and started learning her new lessons on the other side; she wanted to experience everything that she had missed all of these years here on Earth. She was making up for lost time!

From what I've seen, a spirit crosses over and is either ready to immediately embrace its new life on the other side, or they go through a joyous adjustment period in which they realize that they are no longer confined to a body. Other spirits felt the need to experience all of the Earthly delights they missed while they were living in a physical body, and according to them, there was no judgment and they could have (or do) whatever they wanted to do at that moment.

Those that were confined to wheelchairs or had a physical disability immediately got up and walked, ran or even danced, because they could! They were amazed that they had all the freedom in the world.

So, rest assured, Heaven is what we create it to be.

With that knowledge, I'm excited to know that when I leave Earth and cross over, I will be in a world filled with unconditional love and laughter: a place filled with more beauty than we can ever imagine!

What Do They Do On The Other Side?

So, once you've crossed over, do you just hang out and visit with the others there?

As I've mentioned, once a person crosses over, they sometimes have an adjustment period. Some spirits take a little longer than others to get used to being free from the confines of a physical body and to understand that all of the emotions and attitudes that they clung to here on Earth are no longer useful on the other side. Once a spirit understands that, they begin their own lessons or training in the spirit world.

You may be wondering exactly what kind of "training" they would ever really need now that they've passed on. That answer would depend on whether or not they learned all of their predestined lessons while here on Earth, and whether or not they will need to continue on in order to perfect them.

From what I have learned, some spirits are much more evolved when they reach the other side, and so their transition period takes less time than it does for others.

I have seen spirits go through the following phases after they have passed on to spirit:

- Everyone visits with those that have passed on before them; however, it isn't a lengthy process, since they are able to embrace the unconditional love at that moment leaving them satisfied instead of longing.

- Some people that pass on need to go through a nurturing process to help them release any hurt, anger and bitterness that no longer serves a purpose on the other side.

- Some immediately take on a "job," like helping others cross over, or taking care of animals, the elderly and children. From this, they gain knowledge and experience to take with them when they come back to Earth for their next life.

Aspirations

In one particular reading, a mother was grieving her only daughter that had passed in a tragic car accident. She was so distraught that her daughter was so full of life and never had the opportunity to realize all of her hopes and dreams. She asked me what her daughter was doing now that she'd crossed over, and I replied that I was seeing her in a white lab coat like a doctor would wear and that she was holding several babies and children. There were also children holding onto her legs. The mother laughed and said that it sounded just like her daughter. She had wanted to be a doctor and work with children. This information eased the mother's anguish at the thought that her daughter would never accomplish her dreams because she had passed away so young. It also helped her to release some of the bitterness that she had been feeling due to the fact that her daughter was killed by a drunk driver.

Learning

During another reading, a man that had committed suicide told me that when he reached the other side, he had much studying to do. He said he would focus on healing and learning so that when he came back in a different body, he would not bring these same issues into his new life. This time, when faced with the same stress he had been dealing with before taking his own life, he would have the coping skills to handle it in a very different way. This, he said, would eliminate the need to repeat the lesson.

At times, our loved ones also have the freedom to come and go as they please so that they may check up on us to see how we're doing with our every day lives.

But, of course, it's not all work and no play on the other side! That's the beauty of being there, there's much to do, yet there's so much love, peace and understanding.

They Don't Hold Grudges

People often tell me during a reading that before their loved one passed away, they had a terrible argument with them or they still had some unfinished business. A client will usually feel left behind and guilty because they never resolved their differences, or they never got the chance to tell their deceased loved one that they were sorry.

It's situations like this that causes my clients the most distress, leaving a trail of guilt and thoughts that their loved ones are still upset with them. There's a fear that because of this lingering anger, they will never communicate with them from the other side, or even worse: that their loved one will not want to see them when they themselves pass away.

I have found this to be entirely untrue! Our human form makes us susceptible to our ego's need to cling to anger and grudges until someone apologizes. Because most of us who have not reached enlightenment are bound by the ego, and even then we still keep a little piece of that anger, hurt and bitterness buried, only to resurface like an old wound at a later date.

Souls that have crossed over have shared with me that once they reach the other side and adjust to the unconditional love that the other side envelopes them in, there is absolutely no reason to hold onto any of the physical emotions that keep up captive in our Earthly bodies. They do not experience anger, bitterness, hurt or even jealously – there is only the feeling of unconditional love.

They do tell me that there are exceptions, and that's usually related to some sadness and heartache their loved ones are going through here on Earth. The sadness, they say, comes from a feeling of helplessness brought on when they know they must let their loved ones learn their personal lessons on Earth.

In those situations, our loved ones on the other side send us their love and positive energy so that we may work through our issues and move into a better understanding of what unconditional love truly is.

Guilt, Anger And Bitterness? Not On The Other Side

I have learned from those that have passed on that when we reach the other side, we no longer are bound by the emotions that we had here on Earth. There's no longer a need to hold on to debilitating emotions such as bitterness, anger, guilt and rage – these are emotions that we experience while in our human form.

Here's what those on the other side have to say about several situations that cause guilt, worry or negativity to those left behind after their passing:

Arguments – So many of clients tell me during a reading that they had a terrible fight with their loved one and that they feel so guilty because they never had a chance to say they were sorry and to make amends before the person passed away. These clients always want to know if their loved one is still mad at them. The answer to this is NO. There is no anger, guilt or bitterness on the other side. I have been assured that these negative emotions are only felt here on the Earth Plane. There is no need to feel such emotions on the other side, where all is forgiven and based on healing and light.

Life support issues – Another misconception on our part is that our loved ones would be angry with us for taking them off of life support. However, those that have been in this situation tell me very differently, they are very happy to have you remove them from the life support so that they may stop struggling to live when they are more than ready to cross over to a world where they are 100% healthy and happy. At times, it is more painful to stay here and witness the sadness in everyone that comes to visit while they are being sustained.

Funeral arrangements – Sometimes families worry that funeral or burial arrangements were not up to the deceased's standards as would have been expressed here on earth. The funeral arrangements and all the details are considered really only for our own purposes. They are meant to help us feel a sense of closure, preparing us to move forward. Again, the answer here is "No."

Division of assets – Are they mad because of how their belongings were divided between the family members? Since there is no need for material belongings on the other side, and there is no longer attachment to the Earth Plane, this becomes a non-issue. What matters more to your loved one is that there is no fighting over possessions.

Cemetery visits – The cemetery is only the physical resting place that holds a person's remains after they have passed on. Just because their remains might be there, the spirit and soul are not confined there. Therefore, when you are there paying your respects, it's really only symbolic, since they are everywhere all the time. In reality, they do not want you to sit and stare at a site mourning them, because death is really the first step to everlasting life!

So, you see, the answer to all of these questions is pretty much the same. Once we reach the other side, everything that might have been of importance here on Earth, suddenly becomes minute.

New Relationships

When a person loses a partner — be it a spouse or in a short-term or long-term non-marital relationship — the last thing on his/her mind is finding another person to spend their life with. But eventually, as the pain begins to soften, most people yearn for another to share their love with.

It seems common that the one thing that holds a person back from doing this (especially if the relationship was long-term) is the guilt they feel when thinking that they are "replacing" the person who has passed on. The feeling that their loved one would be upset that they actually found happiness once again with another person can prevent someone from moving on with life.

That is far from the truth! In fact, our loved ones want us to live a very full and happy life — whether *they* are here with us, or on the other side. It would make them sad to see us hurt, angry and depressed each and every day knowing that there is someone else in the world that would help make our lives happier and brighter.

Often times, a spirit will connect during a reading to tell the client that they want them to begin to move forward and find another person to share their life with. Their message usually includes that they will see them on the other side, but until that time comes, they want them to get back into the swing of life and start to live and love once again. Because our loved ones care for us so much, they often help us by arranging connections with people that they feel would make good partners for us.

So, even when their partner has connected with another special person, it could be said that they are never too far away.

Don't Waste Your Time Being Angry Or Getting Revenge

When we have a loved one taken away from us through an accident or a traumatic event such as a murder, we tend to be angry at the person that "caused" the death.

So many times, the family of the deceased is so angry that it wants justice and revenge on the person that was at fault. Because more often than not, our loved ones are "taken" away from us before we are ready for them to leave, we hold onto the anger and want revenge.

What we don't realize, is that when a person passes away, it is *their* time, *their* place and *their* destiny – there really are no accidents. Technically, an accident may have occurred, but the timing, location and nature were settled before this person ever came to Earth.

When a person passes, they suddenly become aware of the unconditional love in their new existence. So, the way they passed is no longer a factor for them – they really don't care, because life is much better where they are!

I know that this may be a bit hard to grasp, but this is what the other side has to say about it:

Peace All Around

I once had a mother come to me and inform me that her daughter was missing. She wanted to know if I told clients both "good and bad news." My response was that if I get the information, the client gets the information. It's not up to me to decide whether they can handle it. She was satisfied with my answer, and we proceeded to do her reading.

During the reading, I tuned into the energy of her daughter, and I told the mother that I did not feel the daughter was still connected to the Earth Plane.

The daughter connected during the reading, and shared many personal facts with her mother. She showed me that she had died from a drug overdose, and that she was in the trunk of her own car, which had been abandoned.

The daughter shared with her mother that she knew her mother had taken a "chunk" of her hair. The mother was shocked that her daughter could confirm this! The mother was also angry, and wanted justice served on the person or the people that had sold her daughter this "hot shot" of drugs. Her daughter described the look and color of the house of where she did the drugs and where she died, she also gave the location of her body and the time frame in which it would be discovered.

Now, this was all fine and dandy, but the most important message that came from her daughter was that SHE was the one responsible for the overdose – that no one forced her to take the drugs and that she didn't want her mother wasting time being angry and spending all of this precious time trying to find out who was responsible. I relayed this information to the mother with the hope that she would eventually begin to move forward with the precious memories of her daughter stored in her heart. I told the mother that I hoped that I was wrong, and that if she brought her daughter into the office, I would gladly refund her money to her.

Approximately one week later, I received a phone call in which the mother confirmed the entire reading – police had found her daughter in the trunk of her abandoned car.

The mother also confirmed that she was found on the day that had been mentioned during the reading. Her daughter had described the house where she had bought and used the drugs, and where she eventually died. However, the people that owned the house had plenty of time to get rid of any evidence; there would be no way of proving that her daughter had been there.

She didn't want any of her family members to focus on her passing, but instead to realize that she was no longer fighting the "inner demons" that she battled for so long. She was finally at peace, and she wanted them to be at peace, too.

Divine Order: How Long Will We Be Here?

When someone passes away I hear people say that the person was "too young" – especially if they haven't even reached adulthood. Or, people will make a comment that the person wasn't sick at all, or that it just shouldn't have been their time to go.

From what I have learned, every spirit knows how many days, weeks, months, and years that it will be here on Earth. He/she also knows how many people they will bring joy to, and how many people they will hurt while they are here; it's all part of the blueprint that we set up before we even step into our bodies at birth.

A person does not consciously remember setting this up, otherwise we would live our life according to exactly when we would pass away, and forego a multitude of the lessons we are supposed to learn while here on Earth.

Here is an example of how one person chose the "Divine Timing" for her life:

Right on Time

One summer I was teaching at a retreat, and a woman that was very loved and cherished had a heart attack during our time there.

While paramedics worked on reviving her, everyone was so upset and stood around sending love and energy to bring her back. When I came upon the scene, I saw her standing outside of her body and she told me to "make them stop" sending energy to keep her in her body. She said that it was time for her to go.

I had never been exposed to a situation where a person was not "legally" dead and was still standing there at the scene. Thinking like an Earth-bound human that I am, I began to have a conversation with her and said that she needed to come back into her body because her husband needed her.

Her reply was that he needed to continue his life mission, which could be done without her. She said she considered the people at the retreat to be her extended family, and she wanted a "grand send-off," so she purposely made sure that it was during this retreat when she made her transition, surrounded by her favorite people.

She then said to me once again, very firmly, "MAKE THEM STOP!"

So, I began to block the energy that the students were sending to keep her tied to her body, feeling horrible – as if I were the one that was "pulling the plug."

It was then that a beautiful cream-colored marble staircase appeared to me out of nowhere. This beautiful lady smiled the most brilliant smile, threw her hand up in the air with a wave like the First Lady, turned and began sashaying up the staircase singing, "Happy trails to you …until we meet again!" I stood there in awe, wondering if I really was seeing what I had just seen and participated in. A moment later, they pronounced her dead.

Everyone at the retreat who knew her so well was blown away with what they had just witnessed. Overwhelmed with grief and sorrow for losing a dear friend, they could not understand how this could have happened and ruined the whole retreat.

After taking it all in and processing what had just happened, I began to explain and relay the story of how she had allowed me to see what was going on and why she had chosen the retreat to transition to the other side.

Even though my explanation did not lessen the heartbreak of her passing, it did help her friends see things from a different perspective and to understand that she chose where she would pass and who she wanted by her side.

Who Is With Us When We Pass

Just as we chose when we will go, we also choose who is there with us. I learned this first-hand.

My Story: Saying Goodbye to Granny

My grandmother, who I called "Granny," had had a stroke and was in a coma before she passed away several years ago. Up until that time, my mom was pretty much her primary caregiver and while we all tried to visit often, it really was my mom that did everything for my grandmother.

We received the phone call in the middle of the night telling us that it wasn't going to be too long before Granny passed, so we probably should come to the nursing home as soon as we could. When we got there, Granny was still on the ventilator. She was in a coma, yet very comfortable. She was already in the final stages and her lower legs were starting to turn pale and beginning to get cold, and we knew it wouldn't be long.

As I was sitting there in her room, the repetitive sound of the ventilator had relaxed me so much that I kept nodding off, and I wasn't even tired! My mom finally told me to go out in the lobby and get some sleep and promised to call me as soon as there were any changes. I reluctantly agreed, I just couldn't keep my eyes open. I lay down and closed my eyes and almost immediately began dreaming.

In my dream, I was lying along side of my grandmother and as I lay down, I told her that I was "so very tired." Even though she was in a coma, I heard her say to me, "its ok, just lie down and go to sleep." As I was laying there with her in this dream, the nurses came in and they were wiping her face down and "preparing" her, getting her cleaned up for her passing.

A few moments later, my mom woke me up and told me that my Granny had passed away. I was so angry and asked her why she didn't wake me up sooner – I wanted to be there when she took her last breath.

It took me a while to understand and realize that in reality, I really was there in her last moments on Earth. You see, my grandmother didn't want me there when she passed; she only wanted my mom there because she was the one that had been taking care of her for the last few years of her life. I know now that it was no coincidence that I kept falling asleep, because Granny helped to make that happen.

And the dream … well, it was no dream. I was having an out of body experience and I really was in bed with her at that moment when she was passing!

PART 3:
Questions I'm Often Asked

When it comes to "the other side," there are quite a few controversial theories about what it's like, and what happens to souls there.

We usually form a picture of the afterlife based on what we were taught as children or what we learned in a religious setting. Through my work, I have found some of these theories to be false, based on what those on the other side have shared with me.

Before I share that with you, I would like to stress that I am not here to influence you or to change your beliefs in any way. I'm only interested in presenting this information to give a different perspective on some of the age-old myths about death and what follows.

Some of this may sound a little unsettling to you – and I know that have been left dumbfounded on many occasions after spirits have shown me situations that firmly went against all I had been taught – but, after considering the following information for a while, it made so much sense to me that I could hardly dismiss it. Eventually, I just let go of my pre-conceived notions and trusted what I was shown, allowing my perspective to be broadened.

The following is one example of this:

Suicide

Myth: If we commit suicide we will "burn in Hell."

Mark's Journey

Mark was raised in a devoutly Catholic family, and espoused many of the church's beliefs, including the idea that suicide is a sin. However, there came a point in his life when regardless of his upbringing, he saw ending his own life as the only solution to his problems.

Mark's girlfriend had broken up with him and he fell into a deep depression – it seemed that things were getting worse by the minute and he couldn't pull himself together. Eventually, he shot himself. Right after he pulled the trigger, he snapped back to "reality" and thought, "My God, I'm going to burn in Hell!"

Mark showed me that as he was traveling down a very dark tunnel, and he was so terrified because he just knew that when he got to the other side, he was going to be sent straight to Hell. Mark's "Hell" was going from Point A, (here on Earth) to Point B, (the other side) and was the greatest Hell that he could experience because of what he thought God was going to do to him for committing suicide.

He then showed me that upon his "arrival," he was greeted by a very big man wearing a long robe and sandals. The man's face shone so brightly that all you could see was this beautiful, glowing, golden light – you couldn't even see his face at all! I knew Mark was showing me what we would consider to be a representation of God, because the energy was so loving and so awesome that I didn't want to leave its presence!

Mark then conveyed to me that God addressed him and said "Welcome my son, come and I will give you rest."

Confused, Mark then said, "Me, God? But, I took my own life." God replied by telling him "Yes you did, I will give you rest, and I'm going to love you and help you heal."

Mark was shocked by the kindness and generosity that God was showing to him. Then God said, "However, you ended your life lessons too soon. After you rest and heal, I'm going to send you back! You will be in a different life and a different family, yet you will be in a similar situation. I hope this time you will make a better more educated decision on how to handle it so that you don't have to go through this again!"

At that time, I was still new to doing readings and connecting with the other side. I also still had quite a bit of my Pentecostal beliefs firmly intact, so this just left me blown away. I had never experienced something quite so powerful in my life!

From that moment on, my views on suicide had changed. I came to understand that God is loving and merciful.

Aborted, Miscarried and Stillborn Children

I wanted to briefly touch base on this subject only because there are so many people carrying around an enormous amount of guilt as a result of a decision that they made in their past.

Now, remember, I am not here to persuade you or condone any decisions that have or have not been made, I am only here to clarify what I have learned about these situations.

I have had many conversations with clients about the guilt they feel from aborting a fetus, and some assured me that they were going to be punished for taking a life and that it was an incredible sin to do what they did. They also felt that the baby was incredibly angry with them for their decision.

I asked God how to best answer one client so that they would feel the peace that they needed in order to move forward in life and make the most of what they now had.

The answer I received from both God and from the aborted children was an answer filled with love, compassion and understanding. This is my interpretation of it, again seen and heard through my own eyes and ears. This is not a case of right or wrong, I only ask that you keep an open heart and mind when reading this:

From what I gathered in our conversation is that God does not condone abortion, however we make mistakes and then we must figure out how to fix the mistake after it is made. He said that he understood that birth would not be a healthy option at that time for the person and that the health and wellbeing of the child was extremely important to him.

Although he was not happy about the abortion, he would rather have that as an end result as opposed to bringing another child into a world that could be very cruel to an unwanted child. It would break his heart more to have that child born to a mother or to a set of parents that did not have the means to take care of the child, or that they might neglect or abuse that child. A mistake made and corrected through this method could be understood once, but not repeated after that.

When I asked a child that was aborted if it was angry that its parents made the choice not to bring it into the world, its answer was an answer of wisdom:

It said that it understood that the choice to abort was not made out of anger, but out of love. It realized that the parent would not be capable of taking care of it physically, mentally or emotionally at this time, and that they were preventing a situation that could result in neglect or abuse. Because of that, the child loved the parents even more!

From what I have learned, children that are lost (meaning through abortion, miscarriage or stillbirth) become part of your spiritual team (spirit guides/helpers) until you (or they) are ready to be reincarnated.

Mommy

In the beginning of my spiritual journey, I had started meditating as often as I could in order to start "training" my mind to let go of the chatter that was always taking place.

During one session at home by myself, I was doing inspired writing (where I went into meditation and then would ask if anyone had any messages for me). Toward the end of my session, I had seen in my mind's eye a pair of twins: one girl and one boy. When I asked them who they were, the answer I received was "my children." I thought to myself "OK, that's weird."

About three weeks later, I was attending a meditation group and while on this wonderful journey, I once again saw the same little boy and girl and asked again, "Who are you and why are you here in my life?"

The answer I received not only stunned me, it blew me away! They said "We are your children that you lost so long ago. We are here to help bring happiness and joy. We are so glad for you to have finally met us, and we call you 'Mommy.'" I sat there crying as if I was the baby, but it was such an amazing experience, because during my first marriage, I had miscarried twins!

This experience helped me to see that I might have lost them physically, but spiritually they were still there and available to connect and communicate with me.

Are They Disappointed with Me?

After a loved one passes away, some people are left with so much emotional baggage that sometimes it's a wonder they are able to "carry" it all and stand up straight.

One of the biggest concerns that they have is whether or not their loved one is disappointed in them for a multitude of reasons.

Some of the typical concerns that have been brought up during a reading are the following:

- *"Are they disappointed because I am gay?"*
- *"Are they disappointed because I'm getting a divorce?"*
- *"Are they disappointed because I didn't finish school?"*

Again, the answer to these questions can all be summarized with one word: NO!

Let's think about this for a minute ... would your loved ones want you to be unhappy, miserable or abused? *Of course they wouldn't!*

We have been programmed to think that the decisions we make in our lives should be first and foremost approved of by everyone around us. That we should stay in a situation at all costs because that's what's "right," according to the world.

We then tend to suppress our truest feelings, afraid to move forward because we might hurt or offend someone. When in all reality, we are the only ones who end up being hurt and angry in the end.

Every time a person asks "are they disappointed in me," the answer always comes back with the greatest love and sincerity, "No, we only want what will make you happy!"

When we are happy, our loved ones are happy for us!

Did They Suffer?

A very common question I'm asked is whether or not a loved one suffered when they passed away.

I think that every spirit has either told or shown me that when they passed, it was a very peaceful event. That even though it looked like they were suffering to us, when they decided that they were ready to leave, they slipped out of their bodies as gently as a soft breath.

Most of the spirits that had died from a tragic accident didn't even feel it when the impact took place. It was so quick that they immediately were thrown out of their physical bodies before they even knew what happened. Therefore, *they didn't feel the impact at all!*

The answer that I received from one spirit about the long, drawn-out moments before they finally passed was this:

I had always been taught that if you suffer here on Earth, then that will ensure that you will go to Heaven. I thought that if I suffered before I passed, it would help to make up for all of the things that I did that weren't so good while I was here and that maybe when I went to the other side, I would definitely go to a better place.

Some of the spirits felt that they had some issues to work out before they had passed away, so they struggled to stay alive until they were at peace with who they were and their actions here on Earth. When they finally felt everything was right, they would let go and could leave the Earth Plane.

The suffering was more of a choice on *their* part than something they were subjected to.

Meeting Up With Others

It's no surprise that people want to know whether or not they will see their loved ones that have crossed over before them when they pass away and reach the "other side."

I have experienced many "reunions" between family members during numerous readings that I have done. From what I have seen, loved ones come and meet and it looks like the biggest party ever!

Those in spirit eagerly wait for their loved ones to take their final breath, and when they do, they are there to joyously welcome them to the other side. Sometimes it may be only one person greeting them, but it can also be an entire crowd.

I have also seen the most beautiful angels greet and welcome a person to the other side. Each and every crossing has been a different and unique event.

PART 4:
True Stories & Miracles from the Other Side

Darcy's Story: Things Happen for a Reason

Dear Kelly,

This past summer a very good friend of mine gave me your information and told me to contact you. I was in deep despair over being falsely accused of abusing my adoptive 13 year-old son after being told by his counselor just the day before that if I didn't "do something," he was going to end up in jail. As a result, I spanked him for the first time ever with a belt on his behind for stealing, breaking and entering, lying, and failure to accept a multitude of other consequences – not only on one occasion, but several.

This punishment happened once, however, my son told authorities that I beat him daily, threw him against walls, punched him, kicked him, and locked him out of the house, and on and on. None of it was true, and he was in counseling, yet no one contacted the counselor to verify his accusations. No one investigated at all. Instead, I was charged with Felony Child Abuse and told "kids don't lie about these things."

My career as a teacher and counselor was on the line. More than 10 years of working in the field of education under my belt, and I would lose both licenses if convicted. I had also been a licensed foster/adoptive parent for 20 years – and now people were viewing me as a monster.

Watching what this experience put my twin 7 year-old daughters through was my biggest nightmare and worst heartache. They were removed from my home along with my son, and I was facing up to four years in jail. I was totally distraught.

By the time I called you, my girls had already been returned to me after living with my sister for two months. I called you, as I said, based on a friend's urging and unsure if I should even do so. On one hand, there are so many people out there who pretend to have psychic abilities that don't, and on the other hand, I have met people who do have those abilities and I respect them deeply. I have pretty good intuition, but when the issue is too close to home, my judgment is clouded. I feared that if you were for real, you may tell me something I didn't want to hear. And I also had the hope that justice would prevail even if it was clouded by overwhelming fear and loss at times.

When we spoke, I got a good feeling about you right away. When you agreed to call me back and do a reading over the phone, I was a little apprehensive about how clear it would be. By this time, my girls were back with me, but my son was not. The charges against me were still pending, and I was awaiting trial. In the meantime, I had been suspended from my job as a teacher and working in the office.

Because I wanted you to "prove" yourself to me, I didn't want to say what was going on. You told me that my friend Tania had told you nothing of my situation, and right away you said you felt a great deal of distress around me. I thought "OK … that's an easy one." You said my job was in question that I was afraid I had lost it or I already had. Again I thought: "easy one." Then you became more specific, and told me there is a dispute over a child – a boy – and then you stopped. You became very quiet, and you sounded disturbed. You asked in a pleading voice "Tell me this child ... forgive me I don't know who he is ... please tell me he isn't in your home, that he doesn't live with you?" I confirmed that he does not, and that was all I would say.

You told me I should not have this child in my home ever again, and that this child is evil. Again, you apologized because you didn't know my connection with him, but then you went on to say that he had plans of making my other children motherless. You asked if I had two younger children. I told you "Yes, twin girls." You told me he was a danger to all three of us and that a spirit was showing you things … a spirit very close to me. That this boy was standing outside of my room with a knife, thinking of harming me. You described the hall, and mentioned that I forgot to set some sort of alarm. It shook me to the core at how could you know this. I could rationalize that my friend told you about my son, even though she told me she did not. I know she was concerned for me and wanted so much to bring me comfort. But my friend had no idea about the fear I lived with, the alarm on my son's door, or anything that had to do with knives. You gave me a snapshot of fears I already had about my son, but would never seriously consider.

I put an alarm on his door, which I turned on at night, because he had been sexually abused before he came to live with me at age 9. He had once attempted to molest the girls when they were younger, but they had been well educated about sexual abuse, and told me immediately.

He had been in and out of counseling since he came to live with me. He would steal things like money and random items, so I didn't want him wandering the house at night. But, there was more to the story which I would only share with his counselor, because I didn't want others to view my son in a certain way: I feared he was stealing our kitchen knives.

By this time, all the steak knives were gone. Once, he told me to take his Swiss Army knife away because he was having evil thoughts. When our kitchen knives disappeared, I questioned him, but (as always) he denied everything.

So, when you painted that picture, I knew it was true. Then you told me a spirit is showing himself to you in a police uniform, and you asked me if that meant anything to me, or if I knew anyone who was a police officer. Then you quickly said "No, it's not that," and asked if I was "in trouble with the law," and I told you I was. You told me this was very strange, and that the spirit was saying he was responsible for your trouble, and that "it had to happen."

He said that my trouble is what removed this boy from my home, and that if this didn't happen; something awful was going to happen to me and my girls. He told you that the boy was going to "make my girls motherless," and that this boy is evil, and that I held on to him to long. He told you that I have had warnings, but I wouldn't let go because my love was to strong for him. However, my love "can't save him." You told me the spirit was my brother, and you asked me when he passed on.

I started to cry, because my brother died of AIDS when he was only 29. He lived with me, and I cared for him the last few years of his life, which were before the AIDS cocktail. He was the closest in age to me of my three other siblings, and one of my best friends.

You told me he had been watching over us all these years, that he was very attached to the girls, and that he said he looks after all of us. He said that one of my twins is very much like him, and that he whispers in her ear, and that she often responds to what he tells her. She is ornery like him, and likes to tease me like he did. He said she knows things she shouldn't know that related to him, and often my family thought he was reincarnated as her. But you said "No, he is very attached to her," and that they are "kindred souls" and that he watches very closely over all of us.

You continued to explain that it was my brother who coordinated these events, and we walked through what had happened that day when so many things went wrong, the day when his counselor told me "grounding isn't enough" and that it might take jail – maybe several times in jail to straighten out his behavior. You told me that the boy – who shows no remorse or guilt for anything he does and has created horrendous stories about other people to get them in trouble – doesn't care who he hurts. My brother told you that there was a good side to the boy; that he was a 13 year-old boy who had been abused and tossed around nine different homes all before the age 9.

It wasn't until after I adopted him that I found out that he failed to bond with anyone and I saw the depth of his sexual abuse by several people. He was like many sociopaths: a charmer. As a special education teacher working with emotionally impaired children, I thought I could save him. My love for him upon adoption was unconditional and other professionals had told me I should rescind the adoption; but how do you give up on your child? I couldn't. For this reason, I was told by you (via my dead brother) that I had to go through the hell I was going through.

So, the day after the counselor told me it would probably take jail to stop my son, I had in my head that I can't let him go to jail. That day he refused to do his chores and he stole more money and lied in the process, I sent him to his room, and I went to mine. I thought about what I should do, and I thought about my brother and I and the silly stuff we did to end up over my dad's knee. I decided that I had to be tough I didn't want my son to end up as the counselor predicted. So, I gave him a few swats then sent him out to finish his chores. I felt so bad – even though he didn't finish his chores and he watched the movie he wanted to see and snuggled with us. I always wanted him to know he was loved.

The next day, we were supposed to go to a party but a friend of mine called with the location and for some reason I never got the message. So we stayed home, and instead my son was outside finishing up chores when his biological sister called.

Normally, I would never let him take a call if he was outside, but she hadn't called in so long. The twin who is my brother's "kindred spirit" convinced me to let him talk on the phone, so I let him. He was on the phone for quiet a long time, and not long after that, the police arrived. They talked to him for well over an hour, I knew at that point he had lied to the police, because next thing I know, I am being arrested.

So, was it my brother who lost the message that would have caused us to go to a party that day? Was it him whispering in my daughter's ear to convince me to let my son take the call? Was it also my brother who arranged for a careless social worker who would fail to do their job and investigate thoroughly before placing the boy in my home? Was it also my brother who matched him with another careless social worker who would place the boy with my sister, who has five younger children?

I originally tried to bring my son back home, but my sister's interference and my son's influence on her (along with the charges against me) convinced me he could never come home. I couldn't understand how my sister could take my troubled son's word over mine.

You told me my brother had also said he had played a part in that, and that I had to sever ties with my son, and that my sister was just a pawn in all of this, so forgive her actions. You also told me that my brother said to tell me that he messed up some lights in the basement by a computer when he was trying to comfort me when the girls were away.

My computer is in my basement, and I spent much time there when I didn't have my kids, and I kept having strange electrical problems. One day, a set of lights just went out. You told me that was my brother trying to comfort me. I thought about all the days I cried alone at that computer and knew it was true – these were things you couldn't possibly know! No one knew those lights were out. I had simply run an extension cord for the computer to remedy it.

You told me that my brother clearly stated I would be found innocent, and that my job was not at risk that all of this hell was to protect me and to have my son removed from my home. I was indeed found innocent, and I did rescind my son's adoption.

Sadly, my sister decided to keep him, but I haven't had anything to do with him for months. My sister and I are attempting to have a relationship in spite of him, and I have set firm boundaries that I cannot (and will not) have anything to do with him. She has apologized for her actions, but says she can't just throw him back into the system … I just pray that he doesn't do anything to anyone over there.

Thank you for bringing me peace in a very difficult time.

Take care and God bless,

Darcy

Saved at the Wheel

During my very first gallery session at a festival in Ohio, a brother that had crossed over connected with his sister and had some very interesting things to say to her.

He started by verifying who his relationship to her, his personality traits, and the type of job he did on Earth, as well as the mode in which he had passed away. He also gave some significant dates: the sister's birthday and his passing.

This spirit was pretty comical, he had some interesting advice for his sister regarding the way she should handle some of the members in their family.

After giving her his message, he was ready to wrap up his connection but not before he confirmed something with her: He had me ask if she had recently had a near death experience while driving, and showed me she wasn't paying attention once behind the wheel and how in order to prevent a fatal accident, he grabbed the wheel out of her hand, just in time.

At that point, the lady let out a very large gasp and was rendered speechless. When she was finally able to speak, she confirmed that recently she had fallen asleep at the wheel as her car headed toward a guard rail that kept people away from a very steep drop – going over would guarantee death. The wheel was jerked out of her hand and she was startled awake just in time to prevent the accident from happening!

The brother confirmed that he was the one who saved her and asked her to please "make sure to get more sleep and to pay better attention to her driving."

The lady was ecstatic with the communication by her brother, and also that he loved her so much that he actually saved her life from the other side!

Natalie's Connection

When my best friend Natalie died at the very young age of 32, I was totally distraught. I could not understand how someone so young (to me that was young, since I am only two years older) who had everything going for her, could just up and pass away! It was such a shock, because I had just gone shopping with her two days before this happened.

When I received the phone call telling me she had died, I got off the phone and immediately went into a full blown screaming melt-down. I stood there sobbing and screaming at her, "Why? Why? Did you die? Why did you leave me?? You were my best friend and we had plans, I have things to tell you and to share with you! Why?"

Out of nowhere, she appeared to me, and she told me that she was tired … that she just couldn't do it any more. At that point I fully understood.

Natalie had been fighting depression for the past year; every day was a struggle for her. She showed me that the situation was like a clock that had been wound too much. The clock's spring had sprung, and it stopped working.

I was stunned by her presence and what she had shown me, however, I was also hurt and angry at her for leaving. At the same time, I fully understood that she was no longer suffering and struggling to get through each day. I was sad for me, yet happy for her that she had found a sense of peace.

Two days later (the day before her funeral) I dozed off in my recliner and was having this beautiful dream which I now understand was a visit. Natalie was there and she spread her arms out as if she were going to embrace me. It was so beautiful and comforting, I didn't want it to ever end! She said to me, "Kelly, go and tell people about the angels! It will be hard, they will not believe you, but you have to keep trying! Go and tell them."

When I woke up, I was in awe, because it felt so real and also because Natalie collected angels. At first, I didn't really understand what she was telling me, but it all fell into place later.

You see, I was in the early phases of my career as a psychic and at the time, and I was still doing readings with the angel and faerie cards. I truly believe that she was encouraging me to stay on my path – no matter if the people around me believed it or not. Natalie always encouraged me and believed that I would one day leave Ford Motor Company to become a full-time psychic.

That night I didn't sleep very well. I knew that I would have a hard time keeping my composure at Natalie's funeral, and I was dreading the whole day. Right before I woke up, I had another dream with Natalie in it. She was floating at first, and then smiled and said to me, "I can fly! I can fly!" and then she floated away. I thought it was strange (again, I'm not too good when it comes to understanding dreams.)

Later that day, I was in line for the processional to go to the cemetery and I thought I would just pull out of the line and head home, since the service had been much longer than I had planned, and I just wasn't up to going to the cemetery. But, my car was totally blocked in and already had the little flag attached to it … not sure of what to do at this point, I went anyway.

At the cemetery after the prayers were said, the most interesting thing happened; the family decided to release several doves. I had seen this done for weddings, but never funerals, so I was very surprised! When the birds flew out of the basket, suddenly Natalie appeared again to me and smiled her brilliant smile and said, "See I told you I could fly!"

I laughed and cried all at the same time, knowing that Natalie truly was happy and totally free!

After the trip to the cemetery, I stopped by the salon where both Natalie and I got our hair done. I sat down and was telling our hairdresser all about the visits I had received from Natalie since she had passed, and all about the funeral. In the middle of the conversation, I suddenly smelled the very unique scent of Natalie's perfume! This particular scent was popular back in the 1980s, and I don't think it's even made any more, so I knew it wasn't anyone but Natalie that was right there sharing in the story!

The whole day was one unbelievable event after another. Knowing that she was right there with me all day made everything much more bearable. This was the first of several visits that I have had with my dear friend from the other side.

Little Brother Takes Over

On a sweltering hot day, Darren found himself in my office under some unfortunate circumstance that later led him to connect with his deceased brother. His work vehicle broke down in our parking lot, and after a couple return sessions in the massage chair, he finally asked for a reading – but not until his brother suddenly began communicating during the massage.

During his reading Darren told me he randomly wakes up in the wee hours of the morning to have coffee "alone," not realizing that it is his brother John who wakes him to make that connection. John was killed in a snowmobile accident where he hit a stump and flew off the vehicle and his inebriated friends accidentally ran him over. His spirit told me a cover-up story was concocted to make it seem like he rolled the snowmobile over onto himself because his friends were afraid they would be blamed for murder. No one in the family believes the story and Darren has been very overwhelmed with the grief, because he feels he could have prevented this if he were there. In the meantime, John's friends are holding this burden, and it has made their lives fall apart. John would like Darren to go talk to these men and let them know that John wants them to let go of the grief and burden. He isn't mad at anyone; he was just as much fault as everyone else that was there that night. To get this message across, John has been trying to get Darren to see me for a while, and it took three attempts to finally make that happen.

Part 5: Things You Should Know

Tips For Getting A Good Reading From A Medium

- Try to relax before your appointment. This creates a better atmosphere for the reading and makes it easier for Spirit to make contact.

- Meditate before the reading to ask specific spirits to attend, and to try to receive answers to questions you have.

- No medium can promise that certain spirits will come through during a sitting, although I have found that often I have been able to successfully "send" out the energy to connect with a particular spirit that hasn't connected immediately.

- Spirit provides evidence of identity in many ways. It can be by a name, description, incidents, relationships, or anything that might be meaningful to the person trying to reach them. Be open to receiving this.

- Some things may make more sense by the end of the reading, or the understanding of the message may come at a later time. Don't be too quick to dismiss something that comes through.

- Let the medium know when s/he is correct.

- The true success of a reading is not always measured by prophecy, but by the guidance it provides. Prediction is possible, but you have the power to change coming events.

- Mediumship is not fortune telling. Please do not approach a reading with a "test the medium" attitude.

- Understand that Spirit comes through in a sitting, first and foremost, to give assurances and love to those left behind in the physical world.

- It is not Spirit's job to make decisions for you about career, love, and related matters, but to inspire, guide, and affirm the reality of life after death. Only you are responsible for your life and the choices that you make.

- The medium realizes when the spirits are gone. Don't try to prolong the reading. You are always welcome to schedule another session.

It is important for you to keep an open mind during the whole process, and to be open to receive whatever messages come through and from whomever is trying to come through. You never know who will connect during your session.

If the person has passed and they know that you have a session scheduled, they understand that they have the opportunity to communicate with their loved ones.

The connection could be from someone you may have not known very well or have not heard from in a long time.

Sometimes our job is to receive the message and then pass it along to someone else.

Experience Journal

We all receive connections from our loved ones, angels, and spirit guides at various times throughout our lives. In general, we are so busy trying to keep up with this fast-paced world and our hectic lives each day, that often we miss the communication.

Here are a few things that you might want to give a little extra attention to in order to become more aware of when the spirit world is trying to communicate with you:

- Approximate time of day or night (often it will occur at the same time)
- Are you awake or sleeping?
- What senses are engaged? (sight, hearing, smell)
- Is this a relative?
- Date of this person's passing (if you recognize the spirit)
- Recurring numbers (on clocks, license plates, etc.)
- Finding feathers, pennies or significant object over and over
- Lights, radio, or electrical surges of any kind
- One-ring phone calls, bells or chimes (with no explanation)

Use the following pages to record your dreams, memories and "connections" with the other side. Many times, the dreams or visions do not make sense immediately, but they usually do at a later time.

Date:

Date:________________________________

Date:____

Date:______________________________________

Date:____

The Most Beautiful Rainbow

As we grow up, we learn that even the one person that wasn't supposed to ever let you down, probably will.

You will probably have your heart broken more than once, and it's harder every time.

You'll break hearts too, so remember how it felt when yours was broken.

You'll fight with your best friend.

You'll blame a new love for things an old one did. You'll cry because time is passing too fast, and you'll eventually lose someone you love.

So take too many pictures, laugh too much, and love like you've never been hurt, because every 60 seconds you spend upset is a minute of happiness you'll never get back.

Don't be afraid that your life will end, be afraid that it will never begin.

Live simply. Love generously.
Care deeply. Speak kindly.
Leave the rest to God.

- anon

"If I can provide a sense of peace, comfort and hope by helping someone connect with a loved one that has passed on, or even bring clarity to a situation that they are struggling with ... then I have done my job."

Kelly MacLeod

Kelly MacLeod is an internationally renowned psychic, medium and author who inspires her audience by connecting them with their loved ones that have passed on.

Kelly provides clients with the messages and miracles from the other side, proving that the spirit lives on forever.

As a psychic, Kelly gives information and significant messages to help with issues that you are currently dealing with, as well as those that may come up in the future.

She has helped thousands of her clients change their lives with the clear guidance and wisdom of her unique gifts.

Kelly is available for individual appointments in person or by phone. She is also available for group/gallery sessions and keynote lectures on spiritualism and metaphysics, including psychic development and connecting to the other side.

Contact Information:

Kelly MacLeod
1-888-KELLY4U
www.kellymacleod.com